RATIONAL RUMINATIONS

JEREMIAH | VOLUME I

Dr. Michael Detweiler

PREFACE

This culmination of daily scriptural rumination was born out of a place of deep pain and great hope, following the loss of my son, Rady Michael at just 24.

What started as a simple pre-dawn sharing with my two brothers (following Young Michael's passing and three weeks prior the passing of my older brother's wife Sue in the fall of 2018) turned into a daily blessing to help us all understand and navigate our shared grief. I then shared them with my children and older grandchildren, then a close brother in Christ who lost his 23 year old son three months after Young Michael. Then with a young dad needing encouragement and it has slowly grow to being sent to dozens of friends and friends of friends in need of encouragement.

After more than five years of writing daily "rumination's" and texting them out, one copy, one paste, and one send, at time, you now hold a portion of this labor of love in your hands.

May these "Rational Rumination's" bless and enrich your walk with Christ as much as they have enriched and blessed my walk with Him in writing them.

- Dr. Michael Detweiler

ABOUT THE AUTHOR

Doc was raised on a small farm in rural central Illinois, raising cattle and loving it, growing Christmas trees and begrudging it. Thankfully, all that work took place outdoors in God's original Cathedral, and he relished in it!

His "rational" approach to physical and spiritual minded "wellness" comes from the only unshakable foundation we will ever know, faith in the Lord Jesus Christ and the direction found only in His Word.

Doc's journey in becoming a "Rational Ruminations Writer" comes from a very broad and quite unique resume. A resume which includes farm hand, landscaper, janitor, carpenter, chiropractic physician, acupuncturist, functional medicine practitioner, rotational grazing rancher of cattle, sheep, water buffalo and a voracious reader.

Having earned his Doctor of Chiropractic degree over 30 years ago he will tell you that he is still working on his Ph. D in life. That advanced degree of life eduction is acquired by traveling through the bumps, bruises, knocks, scrapes, challenges, trials, and tribulations in life, and keeping our relationship with Christ out front. As his beautiful bride, Dr. Susan Detweiler, will tell you, "our journey through life towards our graduation to Jesus is a process of progress, not a pathway of perfection."

Doc currently resides in the Ozark's of Missouri managing a 4,000 acre regenerative organic ranch, grazed by cattle and Water Buffalo. He is the father of five, papaw to six and the most blessed man around being married to a Proverbs 31 lady!

His prayer is that these "Rational Rumination's" bless, encourage, uplift and humor you. And most importantly, may they point you towards a vibrant and living faith in Jesus Christ, and a desire to dig deeply into the rich spiritual soil of His Word for your nourishment and sustnance.

DEDICATION

First and foremost, this book and every Rational Rumination I write is dedicated to my Lord and Savior, Jesus Christ! Without Him I truly can do nothing! Secondly, this book and every one to follow is dedicated to the memory of our son Rady Michael.

Rady Michael will forever be remembered as Young Michael to our family, because from our earthly perspective he was called home to heaven far too soon, we love you son!

Losing a child seems out of the natural order of life to any parent who has had to experience the immense loss and deep pain of letting go of a child. When you bury a child you bury a huge piece of your future. Many hopes, dreams and future expectations are crushed. The very weight of the coffin is so heavy that it seems impossible to lift and carry to the cemetery, and it is, without Christ. Praise be to God for taking that weight and making it His burden to carry. Susan and I can assure you that it has been only our faith in Jesus that has equipped us to get up and moving forward each and every day since that cold November morning in 2018.

My writing each of these ruminations before dawn and my bride's faithful early morning editing, is a labor of love and hope of our future in Heaven with our Savior and the reunion one day in glory with Young Michael worshipping the Lord!

I dedicate each of these ruminations to our children Molly, Riley, Michael, Levi and Teodora, and to our grandchildren Jaxon, Jaden, Julia, Brielle, Ronan, and Jameson. God bless each of you and your walk with the King of Kings!

Thank you Teodora for your astute eye in capturing all of the incredible photo art that adorns this and every Rational Rumination yet to come, keep capturing all that beauty. A special thanks to my brothers Alan and Eric whose early morning sharing of scripture after Young Michael's passing served as the catalyst of these ruminations. I especially want to acknowledge and thank Chase Lauer whose talents, skills and tenacity to take my early morning ruminations and transform them into the book you now hold in your hands. I am humbled and grateful my brother. A huge shout out to Bethany Ferraro for selflessly transforming hundreds of archived Rational Rumination texts and transforming them into the pages you read, God bless you young lady!

Lastly, a special thanks to my brothers in Christ, John Ferraro, Murph Lauer and Eric Johnson for coming alongside of me from the day Young Michael passed and being stalwart sources of strength. I thank God for each one of you!

Lastly to you the reader I want to give you the following blessing; "The LORD bless you and keep you; The LORD make His face to shine upon you, and be gracious unto you; the LORD lift up His countenance upon you and give you peace." Numbers 6:24-26

Now let's get ruminating!!!

"Before I formed you in the womb
I knew you; before you were born
I sanctified you; I ordained you a
prophet to the nations." Then I said:
"Ah, LORD God! Behold, I cannot
speak, for I am a youth." But the
LORD said to me: "Do not say, 'I am a
youth," for you shall go to all to whom
I send you, and whatever I command
you, you shall speak. Do not be afraid
of their faces, for I am with you to
deliver you," says the LORD.

Jeremiah 1:5-8

Jeremiah 1:5-8

I GOT YOU

Interesting isn't it, how Jeremiah sounds a lot like Moses in Exodus when God spoke to him through the burning bush.

Moses and Jeremiah both told God that they were poor public speakers, God's response? "Well cowboy up, buttercup Do you remember who made you in the womb of your momma? Oh yeah Me!!!" (My tweak) "Saddle up and carry out my orders 'Private Moses and Private Jeremiah', since I am sending you, I will deliver you!"

I am a huge John Wayne fan, I can thank my dad for that! He introduced me to the Duke at a young age. He and mom would allow me to stay up past my 8:00 bedtime on special Friday or Saturday nights to catch the Duke on our black and white TV (I thought all of John Wayne's movies were filmed in Black and White until we got a color TV when I was about 12)! Didn't matter if the movie was in color or not, the Duke was larger than life and sat tall in the saddle for right and took care of the dirty dogs in the wrong!

When I read these verses this morning in Jeremiah it made me think of the following quote John Wayne actually made, not in a line of a movie;

"Courage is being scared to death, but saddling up anyway."

God knows we are scared, He knows we are worried about the outcome/results/barriers/pit falls etc....before we are even conscious of any of them. Remember "Before you were born I sanctified you...". Sanctified means He set us apart, He built us for our life's work, He put the "dealer package" together just right in our "chassis" before He put us in His custom made "womb factory"!!!!

Let's make our prayer the following today, I just did!

Oh God, please forgive me for being afraid to carry out Your orders in my life! Give me the courage to "saddle up anyway" and take the next step!!! In Your power Father, in Your Power!!!!

Amen, now saddle up!!!

Take a few moments to reflect on a time when you felt God calling you to do something that seemed beyond your abilities. Perhaps it was a task, a conversation, or a step of faith that made you feel inadequate or unprepared. How did you respond to that call? Did you hesitate or move forward despite your fears?

I GOT YOU

_____

_____

_____

_____

_____

_____

_____

_____

_____

_____

_____

_____

_____

_____

_____

_____

Then the LORD put forth His hand and touched my mouth, and the LORD said to me: "Behold, I have put My words in your mouth. See, I have this day set over the nations and over the kingdoms, to root out and to pull down, to destroy and to throw down, to build and to plant."

Jeremiah 1:9-10

Jeremiah 1:9-10

BE YE REMODELED

God is literally putting His Words into Jeremiah's mouth, He has literally set him in the exact position and place that He wants Jeremiah to be so he can go before His people and call them out!!!!

Look what God tells Jeremiah, "root out, pull down, to destroy, and to throw down," then "build and to plant."

I have worked on remodeling houses/rooms and when a major renovation is done you generally need to tear things down to the "studs," the literal framework, before you can rebuild and finish the remodel.

Build; To exercise the art, or practice the business of building. To construct, rest or depend on as a foundation; as, to build on the opinions of others. (Websters 1828).

God is in the art of building! He specializes in remodeling, reconstructing and restoring broken lives, broken relationships, broken churches, broken societies. He is our foundation that does not move, crack, shift or break away.

May we seek God from our own volition to be remodeled and not be stiff necked and stubborn and have to experience some really tough stuff to be remodeled. Remodeling our lives can be very painful (speaking from experience unfortunately), but if we see growth in our relationship with our Savior from the "remodel" it's worth it!

Think about an area in your life that feels broken or in need of change. It could be a relationship, a personal habit, or even your spiritual life. Where do you sense God wanting to "remodel" you, to tear down what isn't working and build something new?

BE YE REMODELED

_____

_____

_____

_____

_____

_____

_____

_____

_____

_____

_____

_____

_____

_____

_____

"I brought you into a bountiful country, to eat of its fruit and it's goodness. But when you entered, you defiled My land and made My heritage an abomination."

Jeremiah 2:7

Jeremiah 2:7

THANKS BE TO GOD

The age old story of mankind (yep that includes you and I) and our wretched sinful self centered hearts.

God rescues us, delivers us, brings us to a good and "bountiful country" and what do we do? Sin, fall away, become self inflated, defile His land and turn to our own abilities and our own selfish interests and desires. Forgetting that we are where we are because of God's Grace, period! End of story!

BOUN'TIFUL, adjective [bounty and full.] Free to give; liberal in bestowing gifts and favors; munificent; generous. (Websters 1828).

MUNIF'ICENT, adjective Liberal in giving or bestowing; generous; as a munificent benefactor or patron.

In general conversation today, "bountiful" and "munificent" are rarely used adjectives. Why is that? I believe it's because we too rarely stop and think, truly ponder in a state of humble awe how God has been so incredibly bountiful and munificent towards us.

Hard to be thankful for what God has done for us, when we are focused on our own narcissistic interests.

By His munificent Grace alone, He provided Jesus, our only path to heaven! Through His bountiful generosity we have been born into this incredible nation, which was founded in His precepts and truths!

Nothing we have in terms of talent, abilities, finances, etc can we take credit for or take for granted. Our very breath is from the generous hand of Almighty God!

Let us daily humble ourselves in thankful prayer to our munificent God for every good thing in our lives! Start with Jesus and His salvation and then outward to our spouse, children, grandchildren, parents, grandparents, our constitutional republic, our vocation, our homes, etc......

Attitude of gratitude!!

————————————————

This week, dedicate time each day to humbly acknowledge and thank God for the "bountiful" and "munificent" blessings in your life. Begin by reflecting on your relationship with Jesus and the salvation He offers. Then, expand your gratitude to include your family, your country, your work, and the everyday gifts you often take for granted.

THANKS BE TO GOD

_____

_____

_____

_____

_____

_____

_____

_____

_____

_____

_____

_____

_____

"If you will return, O Israel," says the LORD, "Return to Me; and if you will put away your abominations out of My sight, then you shall not be moved. And you shall swear, 'The LORD lives, In truth, in judgement, and in righteousness; The nations shall bless themselves in Him, and in Him they shall glory."

Jeremiah 4:1-2

FORGIVEN AND RESTORED

Israel has "backslidden" as Jeremiah states numerous times in chapter 3 (3:11, 3:12, 3:14) from a true faith, obedience and devotion to God.

Backslide; To fall off; to apostatize; to turn gradually from the faith and practice of christianity. (Websters 1828)

Apostatize; to forsake principles or faith which one has professed.

The miracle of God's love is that even when His chosen people have completely turned away from their roots of faith, and forsaken the very foundational principles they once followed, God will take them back if they truly repent!

This verse is so encouraging! So uplifting! So hopeful! God forgives, God restores, God is in the business of bringing back to Him, the repentant backsliding sinner!

I was reminded this weekend of the story of the Russian pianist Maria Yudina (I heard this story on Paul Harvey's "Rest of the Story" program many years ago). Maria never recanted her faith in Christ and even professed it directly to Joseph Stalin himself!

It is mind boggling to think that Stalin, a man responsible for the death's of literally millions in his Siberian Gulags could ever have a chance to enter heaven. But yes even Stalin had that chance.

Maria witnessed openly in writing to Stalin and lived! Please read the whole story at the following link:

https://www.classicfm.com/discover-music/latest/maria-yudina-stalin/

When Stalin collapsed from a stroke in his luxurious apartment inside the Kremlin and laid their for a long while before he was discovered, his private recording of Maria's playing Mozart's Piano Concerto No. 23.

Did Stalin lay there and repent? Did he come to faith in Jesus Christ? Will the butcher of millions be in heaven one day when we arrive? Only the love of Christ could cover Stalin or our sins, and that love is big enough to do so!!!

Backslidden? Repent and return to Christ! He is waiting with open arms!

Unsure of your salvation? Read and believe, 1 John 1:9.

Our Big God with Big love wants you!!

––––––––––––––––––

Take a moment to identify one specific area where you need to repent and return to God. Write it down, and then intentionally commit to turning away from that sin or distraction. Pray for God's forgiveness, using 1 John 1:9 as your foundation, and trust in His promise to restore you.

FORGIVEN AND RESTORED

_____

_____

_____

_____

_____

_____

_____

_____

_____

_____

_____

_____

_____

_____

_____

"Set up the standard toward Zion. Take refuge! Do not delay! For I will bring disaster from the north, the great destruction."

Jeremiah 4:6

ARE YOU READY?

God is warning Israel about the impending destruction coming to them for their leaving Him and following their own evil ways!

The Bible is 100% accurate and true! God does what He says he will do! He does rescue, He does forgive and He does carry out His justice that He says he will!

People have walked away from God today just as they did in Jeremiah's day. Look at Daniel, look at Revelation. God is kind enough to warn us of what is coming (His wrath is coming). Our Savior is coming! God is loving enough to tell us all this just as He did in the time of Jeremiah to repent, come back to Him before destruction comes.

This life we enjoy is not forever, and it is not our final home. News flash, life is 100% fatal for us all!

Whether we die in our sleep during a time of national peace or during a time of Great War or perhaps famine, or occupation etc. or from judgement on our nation by God for our walking away from Him. We all one day will die, unless of course we are alive and raptured by Christ at the time of His glorious second coming.

We are a ridiculous and foolish people, we are warned of an impending winter storm and rush out and raid the stores buying up all the bread and milk (which I have never understood, I don't even like milk toast, or do we just sit in our houses snowed in eating plain bread with a cup of milk?). I was raised to have a freezer and pantry well stocked to avoid all the knuckle heads out raiding the stores at the last minute.

Being prepared is the point. Be in right and true communion with God through Jesus (have your spiritual pantry and freezer full)! Don't be caught by surprise, you may not have time to rush to "the spiritual store" for provision at the last minute.

We don't know when Jesus is returning but He is!!! Be ready, you will sleep better and not be fearful or worried. I have never regretted having a full freezer and pantry, physically or spiritually!!

———————————————

Take a deliberate step to "stock your spiritual pantry." Identify one area of your spiritual life that needs strengthening — whether it's deepening your prayer life, increasing your time in the Word, or reconnecting with a church community. Make a plan to focus on this area, ensuring that you are spiritually prepared for whatever may come.

ARE YOU READY?

_____

_____

_____

_____

_____

_____

_____

_____

_____

_____

_____

_____

_____

_____

_____

"For My people are foolish, they have not known Me. They are silly children, and they have no understanding. They are wise to do evil, but to do good they have no knowledge."

Jeremiah 4:22

GROW UP

I have written in the margin of my Bible next to verse 22, "rebellious little brats." Does that fit much of today's adult behavior? It does in my opinion.

Adults literally demanding to get their own way, too often for no rational reason whatsoever. Just because it is what they want. They will often not listen to, or tolerate any questioning of their stance on or about the topic at hand. They often get audibly louder, refusing to be rational or reasonable, literally pouting and shouting down anyone confronting them or questioning their views.

Much of this in my opinion arises from the fact that as children they were allowed to always be right, seldom if ever confronted when misbehaving, and suffering minimal if any discipline or consequences when they did. They were not raised in the admonition of the Lord and His Word!

Look again at verse 22, God speaking through Jeremiah calls these rebellious adults, "silly children", with "no understanding", "wise to do evil", but to do good (what is right and proper and civil) they "have no knowledge."

If we have not been trained to "The Book" i.e. the Bible, to the rational, reasonable and right truths found in scripture we will have a society of fools! We will lose civil and right behavior and debate. We will lose the ability to rationally problem solve. We will lose all perspective on right and wrong. We will shun the very existence of Truth!

God has and will again "spank" His rebellious children. Let us repent and return to His Word before it is too late!!

_____

Reflect on your own understanding and behavior. Are there areas where you've been "wise to do evil" or where you've lacked the knowledge to do good because you've strayed from God's Word? Consider how well you know and apply the teachings of the Bible in your daily life.

GROW UP

"Declare this in the house of Jacob and proclaim it in Judah, saying, 'Hear this now, O foolish people, without understanding, who have eyes and see not, and who have ears and hear not: Do you not fear Me?" Says the LORD. 'Will you not tremble at My presence….."

Jeremiah 5:20-22

Jeremiah 5:20-22

THE COFFEE IS BURNING

Reading these verses makes me think of the old idiom, we have all heard and likely said, "Wake up and smell the coffee."

"Wake up and smell the coffee is an admonition to face the truth, pay attention to what is going on around one, to accept reality. It came into popularity in the 1940's and widely popularized by advice columnist Ann Landers in the 1960's and 70's." (Online research, Grammerist. com)

I have used this phrase often and still do at times, it fits so much of what is going on in our country today! For example Kirk Cameron (Christian actor and author) having to fight for the right to read his children's book in public libraries. It is a book about teaching character qualities such as "biblical wisdom and the fruit of the spirit, which is love, joy, kindness gentleness, faithfulness, self control." Wow! That all sounds like terrible things to teach our kids now doesn't it?!

These same libraries have embraced drag queens reading during story hours! (As Earl Pitt's would say "Oh good grief, wake up Umerikah!). Over 2,000 people showed up for the first public story hour reading, more than any reading in the 130 year plus history of the library. Some of America is waking up!!!

When I lived in Texas I used to listen to the daily installment of "Earl Pitt's satirical redneck commentary entitled "Wake up America" on the radio station 95.5 "The Range" which was owned by Willie Nelson.

Earl's character would go on a rant about some ignorant, ridiculous nature of some topic of nonsense that was becoming common and accepted today.

I usually agreed with ole' Earl and his redneck common sense approach to life and the topic at hand.

Jeremiah is saying the same thing here, WAKE UP and smell the coffee Israel, house of Jacob! Open your eyes and your ears people, God is speaking!!!

The citizens of this Biblically founded nation, better wake up, stand up, and fight for the constitutional rights of what our nation was founded upon! Fight and vote with our dollars! Let's buy Kirk's book for our children and grandchildren, write a letter to the company's that promote "woke" anti-Christian values and tell them why they are not getting anymore of your money! Share in a kind and loving but firm way why you believe The Bible and it's soul saving Gospel to those all around you!

Wake up America, the coffee is burning!

———————————

Reflect on areas in your life where you may be "asleep" to the truth of what is happening around you, particularly in relation to your faith and the values you hold dear. Are there issues in your community, nation, or even within your personal life where you need to "wake up and smell the coffee"?

THE COFFEE IS BURNING

"Thus says the LORD: 'Stand in the ways and see, and ask for the old paths, where the good way is, and walk in it; then you will find rest for your souls.' But they said, 'We will not listen.'"

Jeremiah 6:16

STAY ON TRACK

This verse is one I have long ago memorized to remind me of where I need to travel in life. Stand firmly on the path of scripture, walking in and on the only place of secure spiritual footing.

When I was 17 years old I had just graduated high school and my church youth leader, John Gerig, took myself and two other guys on a 4 day backpacking trip down the Rogue River in southwest Oregon. The scenery was incredible as we hiked along the river, no tents just our backpacks and sleeping bags, with only the food we carried with us.

We watched kayakers shoot the class 4 rapids, where the 1975 classic Western "Rooster Cogburn" was filmed featuring John Wayne and Kathryn Hepburn. Someday I would like to kayak the river!

At one point of the hike we were several hundred feet above the river along the crest of the vertical cliffs overlooking the river. The path was quite narrow, just wide enough for you and your backpack, one misstep and it would have been over! We took our time and focused on one foot in front of the other and managed just fine. We stayed on the path!

That is what I think of when I read and recite this verse. Stay on the path of faith in Christ, His word is my "big picture" map and will lead me home to heaven one day. It is also my "in the moment map", what I need right now to keep me grounded and focused on what eternally matters.

Have I taken my eyes off the trail? Yes, and I have the scars to show for my wandering too. I return to scripture (my map), repent of my sin that caused me to stumble, pick my self up and get back on track!

Pick up your Bible and get your spiritual bearings dialed back in, and stay on track!!!!

––––––––––––––––

Reflect on your spiritual journey. Have you stayed on the narrow path of faith in Christ, or have you wandered away, distracted by other pursuits? Think about the times you've taken your eyes off the trail and the impact it has had on your life.

STAY ON TRACK

"The word that came to Jeremiah from the LORD, saying, "Stand in the gate of the LORD's house, and proclaim the the word, and say 'Hear the word of the LORD, all you of Judah who enter in at these gates to worship the LORD!'"

Jeremiah 7:1-2

Jeremiah 7:1-2

WEAR IT OUT

At first glance this command seems pretty unnecessary doesn't it? God tells Jeremiah to go to church and "proclaim", which literally means to loudly cry out to all the parishioners entering to "listen to God's word!"

We know from reading this far in Jeremiah that God's people had wandered far from God, so far from His ways and precepts that God had to call Jeremiah to warn them of the impending destruction headed their way. They had literally turned to every falsehood imaginable rather than to God, (Jeremiah 3:26-37).

This falling away from God all happened when the church (actually the Synagogue) was still the central focus of the of the culture of Israel. If this could happen then, how much more likely is this too happen (and has) today?!

So, if this command, this proclamation to "Hear the Word!" by Jeremiah at the gate into the Synagogue for the Israelites was important then, how much more critical is it now?!!!

The Gideon's ministry has given away Bibles since 1908. You know the ones that are in Motel and Hotel room night stands? They have also handed them out in front of schools (at least they used to be). The Gideons gave away more than 70 million Bibles last year, and more than 2 Billion copies since their founding!!!

It is estimated 85% of U.S. households have a Bible and of those that do, they on average have 4.3 copies per home (not sure if that .3 is from the New or Old Testament :-).

The real question is, are the covers of our Bible's worn, are their pages marked up and frayed from being read? Your Bible should feel as good in your hands, as your favorite pair of boots on your feet or your favorite blue jeans when you put them on!

Is your Bibles taken to Church? Do our kids and grandkids know how important it is to you?

Does the pastor of your church open the Bible and boldly preach and teach the whole Word of God every week?

Without the Word of God, can church, really be called church? Let's assess the church we attend. Is the Word of God the center of its existence? Do they peach and teach the whole word of God, even the "culturally sticky parts"; marriage is one man and one woman, God created everything in 6 days and rested on the 7th, Jesus Christ is the Messiah and He is the only way?!

God's Word, is the literal central theme of life!

––––––––––––––––

Reflect on your own engagement with the Bible and how central it is to your life. Do you treat God's Word with the importance it deserves, both in your personal study and in how you share it with others? Consider how you can be more like Jeremiah, boldly proclaiming the need to "hear the Word of the Lord."

WEAR IT OUT

_____

_____

_____

_____

_____

_____

_____

_____

_____

_____

_____

_____

_____

_____

"But this is what I commanded them, saying, 'Obey My voice, and I will be your God, and you shall be My people. And walk in all the ways that I have commanded you, that it may be well with you.' Yet they did not obey or incline their ear, but followed the counsels and dictates of their evil hearts, and went backward and not forward. Since the day that your fathers came out of the land of Egypt until this day, I have sent to you all My servants the prophets, daily rising up early and sending them. Yet they did not obey Me or incline their ear, but stiffened their neck. They did worse than their fathers."

Jeremiah 7:23-26

Jeremiah 7:23-26

FORGIVE ME NOT

God's way is simple, bend your knee to Him, repent of your sin, and He will forgive you of your sin and provide you the newness of life that only can come from His love!!!!

Pretty straightforward right? Are we are not just as guilty as the children of Israel on forgetting God and turning away? God points out His love and presence through that subtle little escape from Egypt that He provided for them from slavery here in verse 25. You know the one, where He literally parted an ocean, allowed His people to walk through on dry land and then collapsed the enormous walls of water onto the ensuing Egyptian army!!!!

We are like, really!!! You can't remember that incredible miracle, and follow that God?!!!

Oh, but wait a minute before we get to judgmental and haughty towards the Israelites let us not forget that we live in a time after the greatest miracle of all times! Christ The Messiah!

We have the complete Word of God, that lays out the facts, including the following; God gave us His only Son born of a virgin, He lived a sinless life, died on the cross, laid dead for 3 days, then rose again, walked the earth for 40 days before literally ascending to heaven!!!!

We have all this and so much more, and we as a society and sadly as a "church" do a pretty poor job of seeking Him with all our hearts don't we?

Look up the following website that lists 351 prophesies that Jesus fulfilled!!

https://www.newtestamentchristians.com/bible-study-resources/351-old-testament-prophecies-fulfilled-in-jesus-christ/

With all of this evince laid out in the Bible we hold in our hands, how can we ever throw a "stone" literally or figuratively at the wayward Israelites in Jeremiah?!

Let us obey His Voice (His Word) today, and take the action step to walk in His ways and enjoy His fellowship.

He will provide the green pastures, the still waters and the peace that surpasses all understanding!!!

———————————

Ask yourself: Are you fully obeying God's voice and walking in His ways, or have you, like the Israelites, been following the dictates of your own heart? Consider how easy it is to forget God's miraculous works and drift away from His commands.

FORGET ME NOT

_____

_____

_____

_____

_____

_____

_____

_____

_____

_____

_____

_____

_____

_____

"So you shall say to them, 'This is a nation that does not obey the voice of the LORD their God nor receive correction. Truth has perished and has been cut off from their mouth.'"

Jeremiah 7:28

DON'T PLAY SPIRITUAL LIMBO

Jeremiah is commanded by God to call out the entire nation for their abandonment of God and His Word of truth! Small job right? One that should go over well and be welcomed with open arms by all, don't you think? Not!!!!

God states in Jeremiah 9:3 that His people "…..are not valiant for the truth on the earth. They proceed from evil to evil, and they do not know Me. Says the LORD."

These verses spurn up within me some deep questions; Have I abandoned the Word of Truth (scripture)? Am I valiant for the truth? Do I believe fully the overwhelming evince of God's Word?

We should ask ourselves deep questions. We should not look at life only through shallow little snippets and sound bites. I believe this is one of Satan's most effective tactic's of our current day and time. Look only on the "here and now", the "immediate", the "latest viral video" or "social media post" etc…

The lack of deep thought and conversations leads to shallow character, ignorance of history, leading to oneself becoming a boat adrift and not one moored and anchored in a safe harbor of truth.

Look again at the children of Israel, how did they become a people worshipping wooden or golden statues and not worshipping the God of creation? By not immersing themselves in scripture, not hearing the spoken word in church, they became self-ish not self-less.

I used the term "evince" yesterday and failed to give the definition; "To show in a clear manner; to prove beyond any reasonable doubt; to manifest; to make evident." (Websters 1828)

Scripture is the proof of God's faithfulness and man's (our) lack thereof. Only by trusting God and acknowledging our need for His son Jesus to be our Savior will we have any success in being faithful to God or live a life with true eternal value!

"Nothing evinces the depravity of man more fully than his unwillingness to believe himself depraved." (Websters 1828 dictionary)

Like I have told all my children and grandchildren; "don't get all loud, proud and self inflated, you're just a skin covered sin bag like everybody else that needs Jesus!"

———————————

Ask yourself: Have you become complacent or shallow in your pursuit of truth? Are you allowing the distractions of the world to pull you away from the deep, sustaining truths found in Scripture? Remember that being valiant for the truth means not only knowing it but also living it out and sharing it with others.

DON'T PLAY SPIRITUAL LIMBO

_____

_____

_____

_____

_____

_____

_____

_____

_____

_____

_____

_____

_____

_____

Thus says the LORD: "Let not the wise man glory in his wisdom, let not the mighty man glory in his might, nor let the rich man glory in his riches; but let him who glories glory in this, that he understands and knows Me, that I am the LORD, exercising lovingkindness, judgement, and righteousness in the earth. For in these I delight," says the LORD.

Jeremiah 9:23-24

GOD GETS THE GLORY

Glory here means to boast or to brag. It is God who equips us with our skills and talents, it is He that arranges our business relationships, He sets the weather in motion to grow our crops and the forage for His cattle on a thousand hills to give a bountiful harvest.

Unlike a former President's 2012 campaign slogan that claimed "You didn't build that. If you've got a business." As if it was only possible to build your business because of his and the governments help. Talk about bragging! I would restate it more like this, "If you have built a business in this country you did that in spite of the government's 'help.'"

Let us only give God the glory! As God shares in verse 24, He exercises lovingkindness towards us, He is the source of all sound and righteous judgement! He provided our Savior Jesus. He alone pardons our sins. Life in its entirety is about God and not us! Tough pill to swallow when we have a myopic view of the world.

Think of the real "Hope and change" that would come about if we all put Christ first! If we truly lived the words of the simple little phrase, "I am second." Imagine what that cultural "reset" would look like?!

All glory, all boasting, all praise be to God alone!

Reflect on where you may be tempted to boast in your own wisdom, strength, or accomplishments. Are there areas of your life where you take credit for success without acknowledging God's role in equipping and sustaining you?

GOD GETS THE GLORY

_____

_____

_____

_____

_____

_____

_____

_____

_____

_____

_____

_____

_____

_____

_____

10)"But the LORD is the true God;
He is the living God and the
everlasting King"

12)"He has made the earth by His
power, He has established the world
by His wisdom, and has stretched out
the heavens at His discretion."

Jeremiah 10:10,12

Jeremiah 10:10,12

THE MAN OF UPSTAIRS

As Christians we worship the One true living God! We do not worship His creation, we do not worship a dead god, a man, or a statue. We bend our knee to The One true God, repent of our sins, accepting and trusting Christs blood as the full and complete atonement for our sins. Knowing that all other roads are literal dead ends with no eternal Hope or peace.

Have you ever been on a trip or move to a new town or area and think your on the right route only to discover that you're on a dead end? It gets really disconcerting when it's pitch dark and you end up on a dead end gravel road with woods on both sides. Then it gets worse when you realize that it is super narrow and nearly impossible to turn around on. I would wager that in that moment, in that eerily quiet spot in the middle of nowhere panic sets in, fear floods in, and for most (even non Christian's) a short prayer for deliverance is sent "to the Man upstairs." How much more scary will it be dying without Christ on the eternal dead end!

Without Christ, and without a relationship with Him, a spiritual dead end is the only road anyone will know. Let us share the road map to Jesus with everyone we come in contact with so they can understand and experience the comfort and confidence of the only road to heaven, Jesus!!

Reflect on your own journey of faith. Are you confidently walking the path that leads to life through Christ, and are you actively sharing that path with others? Consider how many people around you may be on spiritual dead ends, unaware of the living God and the only true way to eternal life.

This week, commit to sharing the "road map" to Jesus with at least one person who may not know Him. This could be through a conversation, sharing a Bible verse, or offering a resource like a book or a Bible. Be intentional about pointing others to the true, living God who created the earth by His power and offers eternal life through His Son, Jesus.

As you go through your week, pray for opportunities to share the hope and peace that come from knowing the everlasting King. Remember that without Christ, every other path leads to a dead end, and let that motivate you to be bold in your witness. Let your life reflect the confidence and comfort that comes from walking with the one true God.

THE MAN OF UPSTAIRS

_____

_____

_____

_____

_____

_____

_____

_____

_____

_____

_____

_____

_____

_____

_____

"For the shepherds have become dull hearted, and have not sought the LORD; therefore they shall not prosper, and all their flocks shall be scattered."

Jeremiah 10:21

Jeremiah 10:21

BE A GOOD SHEPHERD

Boy does this fit the church of America today doesn't it? We have local "churches" and major denominations allowing deeply unbiblical stances to become "church policy/doctrine". Where are the men in the pews? The men that should be literally standing up with the Bible in their hand and finger on the passages during the services and saying whoa their "cowboy i.e. preach, you are out of line!" Boy wouldn't that be a scene? I think we would see some squirming preachers get a bit fidgety and nervous if they were questioned, "how do you reconcile _____ with Gods word?" We must stand on His word and not back down!

I made a business trip this week and had some great conversations with some fine young fathers (one who will be a first time to be daddy this year). I have known two of these young fathers since they were teenagers, and it was such an encouragement to see them growing in the Lord and standing boldly on the Word of God for their families!

This passage made me think of them and how we as fathers and husbands must actively and purposely take the role of shepherding our family flock. We cannot abdicate our responsibilities to be the priest/pastor/preacher of our homes to Sunday church and Sunday school and think "got that one covered".

The young fathers I met with do attend good Bible teaching and preaching churches but also have taken it upon theirselves to teach the Bible in their homes. I know none of them are perfect men and would readily admit and confess that they are not. Boy I sure am not, and have confessed that to my kids and my bride and asked their forgiveness for dropping the ball way too often over the years.

May we all; man or woman, single or married be bold and confident in one thing. The Gospel of Jesus Christ! Let us not allow ourselves or our "flock" to be scattered because we failed to lead and shepherd!

As a guy who has had the "privilege" or better said the frustration of putting sheep back in their proper pasture when they get out. It is much easier to keep them (by checking fences, protecting them with good dogs so they don't scatter by coyotes, etc) than try and get them back in! I can also tell you sheep are far easier than goats to get back in once scattered!

That is a theme that will preach! A wandering sheep is easier to get back on track than a lost goat for sure, but it's best to never wander and get lost in the first place!!

———————————

Reflect on your role as a spiritual leader, whether in your family, community, or church. Are you actively seeking the Lord and standing firm on His Word, or have you allowed complacency to dull your heart? Consider how your actions (or inactions) impact those you are called to shepherd.

BE A GOOD SHEPHERD

_____

_____

_____

_____

_____

_____

_____

_____

_____

_____

_____

_____

_____

_____

"Then the LORD said to me, "Proclaim all these words in the cities of Judah and in the streets of Jerusalem, saying: 'Hear the words of this covenant and do them.'

Jeremiah 11:6

Jeremiah 11:6

DO OR DO NOT!

In Romans 2:13,14, Paul states:

"For not the hearers of the law are just in the sight of God, but the doers of the law will be justified; for when Gentiles, who do not have the law, by nature do the things in the law, these, although not having the law, are a law to themselves."

I have never been a Sci-fi movie or book fan, now give me a Louis L'Amour, Larry McMurtry book or a John Wayne movie and I am all in. My bride is a Sci-Fi fan and one of her favorite quotes is from Yoda, in Star Wars episode 5 'The Empire Strikes Back'; "Do or do not. There is no try." I thought of that quote when I read Jeremiah 11:6 "….Hear the words of this covenant and do them."

After we come to Christ, receive His forgiving grace and have been transformed and renewed by the indwelling Holy Spirit we should be inclined and motivated to be a 'doer' not just a 'hearer' in a sincere application of living as Christ would want us too.

We have the new covenant of Jesus Christ through His Blood and as such we are free from having to obey and follow the 'letter of the law'. The law is our teacher to show us that we are incapable of following it to "earn heaven", and why we need Christ as our complete propitiation/satisfaction to forgive us of all our sin.

I like the following quote from my Nelson study Bible on Romans; "'by nature do the things in the law': Gentiles (non Jews) who do not have the Law still do such things as honor their parents, which indicates that they believe in a basic moral law. They know within their hearts that there is a difference between right and wrong. This "law of conscience" serves as a judge to them in place of Moses' law."

We all possess a magnetic pull towards right, we root for the little guy that the bully is picking on when they duke it out, we cheered when the Allied Forces defeated Adolf Hitler and the Germans, maybe just a little when the Cubs won the World Series (big deal for a Cardinal fan).

Let's live like a Christian should; being doers of good, sharing the hope of Christ, uplifting the hurting in prayer and action, honor our parents, donate our money to charities and organizations that truly make a difference for Christ and good not just 'sound like they do' which requires our due diligence.

Do!

Reflect on how well you're living out your faith. Are you merely hearing God's Word, or are you actively doing what it commands? Consider whether your actions reflect the transformation that comes from knowing Christ.

DO OR DO NOT!

_____

_____

_____

_____

_____

_____

_____

_____

_____

_____

_____

_____

_____

_____

"Righteous are You, O LORD, when I plead with You; Yet let me talk with You about Your judgements. Why does the way of the wicked prosper? Why are those happy who deal so treacherously? You have planted them, yes, they have taken root; they grow, yes, they bear fruit. You are near in their mouth but far in their mind."

Jeremiah 12:1-2

Jeremiah 12:1-2

GET REAL WITH GOD

Jeremiah is talking with the Lord as he would with a really good close friend, very frankly and openly. He is humble and respectful as he should be, but lays out the trouble on his heart.

We need that kind of open, honest, raw and real kind of relationship with God in each of our lives too. "Lord I love you, Lord I know you are in total and complete control, I need to chat with you about _____ issue or injustice or challenge I am facing or I see today.

Talk it out with Him, lay out the details, tell Him your burden and even share with Him how you could see Him level the playing field. Jeremiah does this in 12:3, "….pull them out like sheep for the slaughter, and prepare them for the day of slaughter." We need to be real and raw with God through our prayers, this unbelievable privilege has been provided to us through Jesus' blood on the cross.

We must always remember God is in control, His thoughts and ways are above and higher than ours, Isaiah 55:8-9. He sees the big picture, the long game leading to Christ's return and Jesus cleaning up this mess here on earth!

When we converse and talk openly and frankly with God we are thinking, and if we pray correctly we will be thanking Him as we think and chat.

As the late Steve Farrar of Men's Leadership Ministries once shared in a sermon at Chuck Swindoll's Stonebriar Church in Frisco Texas that we attended when we lived in McKinney; "Christianity is a thinking and thanking faith, the only 'religion' that involves thinking. We were built in God's image and from that design are built and equipped to think, and if we really think, we will inevitably arrive at thanking Him." (My paraphrase). Steve was amazing at drilling down to fundamental truth's of scripture! I will find the copy of that sermon again I have in a file and be refreshed when I do! He went to the Lord a few years back but left a great Godly legacy!

Let's chat with God, let's think and share openly and let's always re-member "Thy will be done, Lord", but it's not wrong to share our thoughts and desired outcome knowing that the ultimate conclusion and outcome is by His hand!

Pray, chat, think and thank God today!!! Jesus opened the conduit to the throne to be used not to sit idle!

———————————

Reflect on your current relationship with God. Are you open and honest in your prayers, or do you hold back your true thoughts and feelings? Consider whether you fully embrace the privilege of speaking candidly with God, trusting that He hears and understands your concerns.

_____

_____

_____

_____

_____

_____

_____

_____

_____

_____

_____

_____

_____

_____

"Hear and give ear: do not be proud, for the LORD has spoken. Give glory to the LORD your God before He causes darkness, and before your feet stumble on the dark mountains,"

Jeremiah 13:15-16

Jeremiah 13:15-16

LISTEN AND GIVE EAR

Hear: shâma', shaw-mah'; a primitive root; to hear intelligently (often with implication of attention, obedience,) Strongs concordance.

Boy have I failed at hearing intelligently in my lifetime! Ask my bride, but I would prefer you didn't because that would be embarrassing. I believe (maybe I should say I hope) all of us would say we have been guilty of not hearing intelligently with the intent to obey in our life-times. If it's only been me guilty of this, then "ouch"!

To "give ear" means to literally lean in with a cupped hand around one's ear so you do not miss a single detail.

That definition gives me the mental picture of an old grandpa, wear-ing bib overalls sitting in a rocking chair on an old front porch. He is leaning his body and his head toward the person speaking, while simultaneously cupping his ear. We all know the scene, the old boy is nearly fence post deaf and the person "speaking" is really yelling and he still can barely hear them. But as the old joke goes, you could whisper, "the cows are out and on the county road" and he will shoot up out of that chair like a bullet while cussing you for yelling at him as he runs towards the barn :-)

God wants us to "shama" Him; to listen intelligently with complete focus and our full intent to follow through on what He is saying.

To "listen and give ear" requires us to fully engage and actively listen to God, or our spouse or child or grandchild etc.

In a world overrun by distractions and constant "noise" we must train ourselves to hear God. It also requires us to open His Word to "hear" what He is saying.

Are we listening to God with the intent to obey?

———————

Practice "giving ear" by eliminating distractions. Turn off your phone, find a quiet place, and approach God's Word with the intent to obey. Imagine yourself leaning in, like the old grandpa on the porch, straining to catch every word, ready to act on what you hear.

After listening, write down one specific action you can take in response to what God has spoken to you. This could be a change in behavior, an act of kindness, or a step of faith. By intentionally listening and then obeying, you'll be giving glory to the Lord and ensuring your feet don't stumble on the dark mountains of disobedience.

Train yourself to hear God with the intent to obey, and let this practice transform your relationship with Him.

LISTEN AND GIVE EAR

1) "Then the LORD said to me, "Even if Moses and Samuel stood before Me, My mind would not be favorable toward this people. Cast them out of My sight, and let them go forth."

3) "And I will appoint over them four forms of destruction," says the LORD: "the sword to slay, the dogs to drag, the birds of the heavens and the beasts of the earth to devour and destroy. I will hand them over to trouble, to all Kingdoms of the earth, because of Manasseh the sin of Hezekiah, king of Judah, for what he did in Jerusalem."

Jeremiah 15:1,3

DON'T PUSH ME

Well they did it! The children of God have stepped on the last nerve of God, they have pushed Him too far. So far that it wouldn't matter if even Moses or Samuel stood and pleaded with Him for a pardon God wouldn't pull back His discipline.

God states He is going to be so complete in His judgement on the sinful, wandering, blatantly disobedient people that He lists what "tools" He is going to use: death, sword, famine and captivity from foreign armies to administer His punishment! Wow, talk about a complete and thorough discipline!!!!

I can remember as a boy on more than one occasion that I and my brother went too far and did not course correct with a simple warning.

Once was on a long vacation road trip and we were at each other in the back seat, pestering and bickering etc. (this was loooong before any media devices were in the car to hypnotize us). We were in the desert somewhere in Arizona, Eastern Colorado, or New Mexico. Dad told us, "that was it, no more or he was going to pull over and get a switch and warm up our rear ends!" I remember thinking, well their are no trees anywhere, so no switch, so long story short we didn't stop our agitating very long. Yep, you guessed it, over went the car to the side of the road and we were instructed out to the back of the car (still feeling confident of no trees, no switch). Well guess what Dad pulled out of the wooden "camping gear" box on the back of our pop up camper? A switch!

He was a man prepared for all contingencies, including a desert with no trees for a switch! He calmly reminded us of our offense and administered our spanking's like any good dad does when he follows through and doesn't just endlessly threaten. We prayed with him while crying and rubbing our rear ends, asked forgiveness for our disobedience and then resumed a now calm and quiet trip, likely listening to some old country music.

Good dad's who love the Lord and love their children are like our Good God. They give us a chance to course correct without a spanking, but if we continue they reign us in! They follow through, and I can attest as a parent that when we follow through with the discipline we do so with a heavy heart knowing we must train our children to follow God and avoid destruction!

Let's submit to God before He has to "pull over the car." He has a switch for Pete's sake He can instantly create a tree to pull one from if He needs too!

––––––––––––––––––

Reflect on the times when you've ignored God's warnings or continued in disobedience, thinking there wouldn't be consequences. Just as a loving parent disciplines their child for their own good, God disciplines us to bring us back to Him and keep us on the right path.

If you recognize an area where you need to course correct, take immediate action to do so. This might involve repentance, changing a habit, or seeking reconciliation in a relationship.

DON'T PUSH ME

"Therefore thus says the LORD: If you return, then I will bring you back; You shall stand before Me; if you take out the precious from the vile, you shall be as My mouth. Let them return to you, but you must not return to them."

Jeremiah 15:19

Jeremiah 15:19

CHECK YOUR POSTURE

The subtitle for verses 15:19-21 is; "The LORD reassures Jeremiah." The Lord lays out the proper sequence for Jeremiah to get back on track with his job as Gods prophet. (Same process for us)

1) Repent and get right with God
2) Then God will bring you back
3) Stand in the way of God, and don't fall into the muck and grime and sinful ways of the godless.

I like what John MacArthur states in His commentary; " Jeremiah had to have the proper posture before God and repent. If he did so, he would discern true values ("take out the precious" a figure drawn from removing pure metal from dross).....Let sinners change to his values, but let him never compromise to theirs. As a man who is to assay and test others, he must first assay himself."

Assay; The trial of the goodness, purity, weight, value, etc. of metals or metallic substances. Any operation or experiment for ascertaining the quantity of a precious metal in an ore or mineral. (Websters 1828)

God is in the purification business, hence the analogy of heating up a precious metal (gold, silver etc) in a very hot furnace/fire and pouring off/removing the impurities/dross that come to the surface. It takes intense heat to purify metal, to literally boil out all the impurities/dross.

We must be always checking ourselves to make sure we are not allowing the world and it's godless values invade and infect God's ways/values within us. Trials in our lives are often the "heat" needed to boil out the dross that has seeped into our life.

Let's assay ourselves, our motives, our attitudes, our pride, our behaviors and confess our issues to God and get back on track with God's plan for our life.

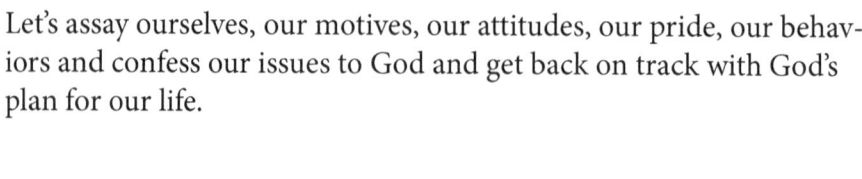

Be vigilant in your walk with God. Reflect on your spiritual state and consider whether you've allowed impurities—worldly values, sinful habits, or compromised beliefs—to seep into your life. Are you in need of a "purification process" to remove the dross and return fully to God?

CHECK YOUR POSTURE

_____

_____

_____

_____

_____

_____

_____

_____

_____

_____

_____

_____

_____

_____

_____

_____

_____

"And it shall be, when you show this people all these words, and they say to you, "Why has the LORD pronounced all this great disaster against us? Or what is our iniquity? Or what is our sin that we have committed against the LORD our God?"

Jeremiah 16:10

Jeremiah 16:10

WHO, ME?

When I read this passage, I immediately pictured a little boy getting caught doing something he knows he shouldn't have been doing by either his parents or a teacher and replying, "Who me?" Even more ironic is that he is the only one in the room when he gets caught and he is in process of committing"the crime", when he gets caught and still proclaims, "Who me"?

It's like the big liberal led cities today that have made deep cuts to the police departments, decriminalized stealing and theft, legalized all forms of drugs, abolished cash bail etc. Then these same leaders have the audacity to decry the fact that stores are closing, major companies are leaving their cities (due to the crimes against their employees working in these cities), high taxes etc. These same "leaders" act like that boy when confronted about their policies driving people and companies away, "My policies?" they are not responsible for people leaving?

"No way! I didn't cause this, it couldn't be! It's those rigid horrible people who believe the constitution is still valid, that there is right and wrong in the world and that we should do such horrible things like punish criminals." "It's those unloving Christian's fault!"

Now those are not all direct quotes of course, but you get the point. Moral relativism (there is no true right or wrong) and there should not be any consequences for evil, deviate wrong behaviors is eroding our country just like it eroded God's people in Jeremiah's time.

Wake up America (let us not forget Earl Pitt's)! We must return to God's ways! Yes love the sinner for sure, but we must enforce the law and acknowledge and punish lawlessness! There is right and there is wrong, there is light and their is darkness, there is good and there is evil. There is one true God, there is His Word and there is always hope in Christ!

Who me? Yep, you too need the hope of a relationship with Jesus!

Reflect on areas in your life where you might be avoiding responsibility for your actions or ignoring the consequences of your choices. Are there situations where you've been tempted to say, "Who me?" instead of acknowledging your role in the problem?

Consider how you can actively return to God's ways in your daily life. This might involve making amends with someone you've wronged, correcting a behavior that you've justified, or standing up for what is right in a situation where others are compromising.

WHO, ME?

_____

_____

_____

_____

_____

_____

_____

_____

_____

_____

_____

_____

_____

_____

"O LORD, my strength and my fortress, my refuge in the day of affliction….."

Jeremiah 16:19

Jeremiah 16:19

THE LORD IS MY STRENGTH

Our God alone is the source of our strength!

Strength: Firmness; solidity or toughness; the quality of bodies by which they sustain the application of force without breaking or yielding. (Websters 1828)

God is our firmness, He is our ability to stand solid with resolute toughness, to be able to sustain the blows of this world and not break or yield!!!

God is our fortress! Websters 1828, defines a fortress as follows: a fortified place; a fort; a castle; a strong hold; a place of defense or security.

Refuge: That which shelters or protects from danger, distress or calamity; a strong hold which protects by its strength, or a sanctuary which secures safety by its sacredness; any place inaccessible to an enemy. Again from Websters 1828 dictionary.

God is our castle and place of defense and under His wings He is literally our secure and safe place that is totally inaccessible by Satan and His minions!!

As you read the rest of verse 19 it describes how the Gentiles would come to God, the God of Israel in fulfillment of Genesis 12:1-3 (Nelson).

We are living in that fulfillment! Jesus completed that promise! For Jew or Gentile alike, Our God through Jesus Christ is our secure place of shelter, our complete and total fortress and castle of hope, our Rock of

Gibraltar, whom empowers us to take every blow this lost world throws at us!!!

Let us stand resolute, unbendable, unbreakable this day and every day hereafter! Stand firm under the wing of Almighty God (Psalm 91:4) and boldly share the path to our fortress through Jesus Christ with the lost around us. They are getting beat up, they are believing Satan's lies and are hopeless and downcast from the weight of a godless present and future!

Strength, fortress and refuge!!!!

———————————————

Reflect on your current challenges and consider whether you are fully relying on God as your strength, fortress, and refuge. Are you allowing Him to be your unbreakable support, or are you trying to withstand the pressures of life on your own?

Let your life be a testimony to the unyielding strength and safety that God provides, and boldly offer the hope of His fortress to those who need it most.

THE LORD IS MY STRENGTH

_____

_____

_____

_____

_____

_____

_____

_____

_____

_____

_____

_____

_____

_____

Thus says the LORD: "Cursed is the man who trusts in man and makes his flesh his strength, whose heart departs from the LORD."

Jeremiah 17:5

Jeremiah 17:5

100% GUARANTEED

Displaced faith and trust is what comes to mind when I read this verse.

I think of someone buying an item like a car part that is "guaranteed for life". The purchaser now has faith and confidence that the part is of quality and durability. Is that faith/confidence justified? Did the purchaser research and thoroughly vet the part manufacturer or the retailer who sold the part? Did the purchaser read the fine print and save the original receipt that may be required for return, perhaps the fine print says the part must be professionally installed and have documentation from the installer, etc.

My point is, the guarantee is only as good as the company that made and backs the part. Has the company earned its reputation? Have they built a reputation by doing what they say they will? I have several companies that I patronize that have earned my trust and confidence by living up to their guarantees. Some small shops with no guarantee in writing at all but have through action and performance long earned my trust. I am sure you have some favorites too.

God is the ONLY 100% rock solid, guarantee you and I will ever know! He sealed that eternal guarantee in blood, the shed blood of His only Son Jesus Christ. He also gave us the only written guarantee that has been and will continue to be accurate for all eternity, His Holy Bible!

The only guarantee written in blood for all eternity, Jesus!!!

————————

As you place your trust in God's eternal guarantee, let your life reflect the peace and confidence that comes from knowing you are standing on the only solid foundation.

Reflect on where you are placing your trust and confidence. Are you relying on human strength, wisdom, or promises, or are you fully trusting in God's eternal guarantee? Consider how easy it is to misplace your faith in things that are ultimately unreliable.

100% GUARANTEED

_____

_____

_____

_____

_____

_____

_____

_____

_____

_____

_____

_____

_____

_____

_____

Thus says the LORD: "Cursed is the man who trusts in man and makes flesh his strength whose heart departs from the LORD. For he shall be like a shrub in the desert, and shall not see when good comes, but shall inhabit the parched places in the wilderness, in a salt land which is not inhabited."

Jeremiah 17:5-6

Jeremiah 17:5-6

FAITH NOT FEAR

We have this picture of the man who puts his confidence in the flesh, his own abilities and in his fellow man's abilities and has no acknowledgement or faith in God.

We are witnessing this every day in society at large! We have lived through a pandemic or better stated a fear of a "pandemic" in the last 2 1/2 years. Those with little or no faith in The Living God, have bowed there knee to the altar of fear and to the false god of man's technology over God's sovereignty!

When we take our eyes off God, when we lose our confidence in Him and His Word, when we transfer our faith from God and put it in man and his abilities we are like that lone shrub in the midst of a vast desert. We are alone even in the midst of the other fear filled individuals on FaceTime or zoom.

We will find ourselves spiritually empty, parched, dried up, dehydrated, brittle and fragile from the absence of the Living Water of Jesus.

Society at large has allowed fear of a "virus" and the faith in "science and government" to rob us of the nourishment of fellowship and living exchange of human touch. Fear dehydrates and dries up our relationship with Christ! We allowed the "experts" to amputate us from the body of Christ! Satan has had a heyday and still does when we elevate man above God!

Faith NOT fear!

Take intentional steps to realign your trust with God and not with human strength or solutions. Identify any areas in your life where fear has taken over due to reliance on man rather than faith in God. Write these down and pray over each one, asking God to restore your confidence in His sovereignty and provision.

_____

_____

_____

_____

_____

_____

_____

_____

_____

_____

_____

_____

_____

_____

"Blessed is the man who trusts in the LORD, and whose hope is in the LORD."

Jeremiah 17:7

Jeremiah 17:7

WHO DO YOU TRUST?

In Isaiah 30:18, it states:

"Therefore the LORD will wait, that He may be gracious to you; and therefore He will be exalted, that He may have mercy on you. For the LORD is a God of justice; Blessed are all those who wait for Him."

I have written in my Bible's margin in direct correlation to verse 7 of Jeremiah 17 on July 7th, 2019 the following, "Praising God, Young Michael's hope was in the LORD, lamenting for our son."

A Christian friend of mine told me that if I didn't still find myself with tears at random moments and times in the weeks, months and years after losing Michael I was lying to myself and not truly addressing the grief within. Well Craig, I still have tears and it's been 4 years and 3 months since Michael went home.

My tears have flowed off and on ever since Michael passed, but now more of the tears are tears of joy and gratefulness than of gut wrenching tears of sorrow that come from the core of my soul.

That is because as I walk along in life I am so deeply grateful that Young Michael had his trust and faith in Christ alone! And I know that my time is shorter today until I get to see him again than it was yesterday. Now don't worry I am not longing to die, rather I am embracing life and am less concerned about dying.

Above all else, I long to be in the presence of my Savior, but I am also anxious to see my Christian family and friends that have already gone ahead especially Michael. To have that skinny little dude hug me again will be a blessing and I may not let go for a few months (hey we have eternity right so that hug might just take that long).

I have had the true honor to care for a lot of people over 90 and many over 100 in my 30 years of clinical practice, with the overwhelming majority being born again, Christ loving believers! Consistently, they shared that they were so excited and anxious to see Jesus and to reunite once again with their family and friends who have already passed and to reminisce once again with them and there shared life experiences.

When we are saved and know our family and friends are saved as well, we have such a beautiful hope! I believe fully that God has a specific time and date for each of us, He won't take us home one day early, but what a glorious day that will be when He does. It is the eternal hope and security of Christ that softens the pain of losing a loved one who is saved, especially when they are young.

Reflect on where you place your hope and trust, especially in the face of loss and grief. Are you anchoring your heart in the Lord, knowing that He is your ultimate source of comfort and assurance? Consider how trusting in God's promises can bring peace even in the most difficult times.

WHO DO YOU TRUST?

_____

_____

_____

_____

_____

_____

_____

_____

_____

_____

_____

_____

_____

_____

"The heart is deceitful above all things, and desperately wicked; Who can know it? I, the LORD, search the heart, I test the mind, even to give every man according to his ways, according to the fruit of his doings."

Jeremiah 17:9-10

Jeremiah 17:9-10

SEARCH YOUR HEART!

The 'heart' from Strongs Concordance is as follows: êb, labe; the heart; also used (figuratively) very widely for the feelings, the will and even the intellect; likewise for the centre of anything.

Wow! Now look at verse 9 again and replace "The heart" with "Feelings."

"Feelings are deceitful above all things and desperately wicked; who can know it?"

Deceitful: Tending to mislead, deceive, trickish; fraudulent; cheating (Websters 1828).

Our "heart/feelings" are wicked and deceitful when our heart has not been transformed by the saving grace and power of Christ and then occupied with the Holy Spirit!

We cannot trust our "trickish, deceitful and fraudulent feelings"! Ever!

We must test our heart/feelings constantly by checking them against God's Word! Use Philippians 4:8 as a filter for everything! If our thoughts, words, actions, deeds etc. don't filter through that verse, chuck whatever it is out with the trash, it is not worth doing!

God says it right here in verse 10, He searches our "feelings/heart", then He says "tests the mind," which is kilyâh, kil-yaw'; in Hebrew and refers to a kidney (as an essential organ); figuratively, the mind (as the interior self):—kidneys, reins. (Strongs)

God weighs out and searches it ALL! Scary right? Forget that song about Santa checking his list on whose naughty or nice, God is doing the deep dive on our hearts!!!

We must be thinking deeply especially on God's Word, and we know thinking is not encouraged in todays world of shallow, emotionally hyped, fear mongering self proclaimed 'thought leaders' that dominate social media and our government.

We need to know Gods Word intimately so we will not be misled by our "hearts" and emotions that are so often fear driven and irrational.

We must develop a stable mind and rational thinking process which can ONLY be found in Christ and the indwelling power of The Holy Spirit!

God and His Word must be our rock!! He is the only immovable, unchangeable EVER!!!!

God is good!

Reflect on the reliability of your heart and feelings. Have there been times when your emotions led you astray or caused you to act in ways that weren't aligned with God's truth?
Consider how often you check your thoughts, feelings, and actions against the Word of God.

SEARCH YOUR HEART!

_____

_____

_____

_____

_____

_____

_____

_____

_____

_____

_____

_____

_____

_____

_____

_____

"As a partridge that broods but does not hatch, so is he who gets riches, but not by right; it will leave him in the midst of his days, and at his end he will be a fool."

Jeremiah 17:11

PURSUE RIGHTEOUSNESS

I was taught/told by more than one old experienced farmer to place a glass egg underneath a chicken to trick her into sitting on the nest and to start brooding eggs to hatch. Not all chickens will fall for the deception but some will and will then start laying eggs in the nest (and you can slip others under her as well) next to that glass egg and as they say "nature will take its course".

It is was believed in the times of Jeremiah that partridges will sit on eggs that they have stolen and when they hatch and grow a bit, the hatchlings will hear the sound of their own kind and fly off and leave the partridge with an empty nest.

Both of these little stories depict deception, one tricking the hen to start brooding by sitting on a glass egg. I wonder how long that hen would sit on that glass egg? Sorry, my mind can wander. The other of the partridge stealing eggs that she doesn't lay and being left with nothing after the young hatchlings grow a bit, leaving her with nothing. The partridge story paints a clear picture from nature for us doesn't it?

We can easily become envious of the shister/con-man who amasses an empire through his scams and hustles. Buying cars, houses, vacations etc. and seemingly "getting away with it". Some times that shister will get caught and lose it all, Bernie Madoff ring a bell?

We all know of many of these shister types that seem to get off scot-free don't we? They live well and die in luxury never seeming to pay a price for their ill gotten gains.

Well the Bible tells us that many will die young and even if they don't when they do die, how well does that fortune take care of their eternal needs? Ever see a hearse pulling a U-Haul trailer or a safe full of money to the Cemetary? If you did I am pretty sure that other thieves and shisters would rob his grave pretty quick.

Look up Luke 12:13-21 and Psalm 55:23 and you will be comforted and clearly reminded that God's ledger sheet will always be balanced. No one will get away with anything even if we don't see the final outcome.

I just read of a famous actor from the TV show Law and Order, who died yesterday in his home in the south of France. His dying words were horrific! Not sure if he was swearing at God or who, but if it was to God and that is what he thought of Christ, his eternity which started the second he drew his last breath, will not be pretty, ever!!! He may have lived a life of the rich and famous in luxury but now it is quite likely not that at all!

Serve God well. Share the good news and the hope of Christ with all. Enjoy all that you have been blessed with and know as a believer, the really good stuff is yet to come.

Forever in heaven!!!!!

Reflect on your attitude towards wealth and success. Have you ever felt envious of those who seem to prosper through dishonest means? Consider how easy it is to be deceived by the appearance of success when it is gained through unethical or unrighteous methods.

PURSUE RIGHTEOUNESS

"A glorious high throne from the beginning is the place of our sanctuary. O LORD, the hope of Israel, all who forsake You shall be ashamed. "Those who depart from Me shall be written in the earth, because they have forsaken the LORD, the fountain of living waters."

Jeremiah 17:12-13

SEEK THE LIGHT

I have recently discovered the Austrian economist and social philosopher Ludwig von Mise, after reading an article in the book "Imprimis: 50th Anniversary Collection" the article is entitled "Coping with Ignorance" by F. A. Hayek from July 1978. Not a light read, but I like that challenge.

Mise was a staunch advocate of the gold standard as well as unrestricted laissez-faire free market advocate and staunch believer in the right of private property. Mise had escaped the Nazi's just prior to WW II, the man knew first hand what a crushing godless government can do!

How does Mise connect to todays passage? Mise was described as being "intransigent" on insisting on a non-inflationary gold standard and his "hands off/laissez-faire"free market approach.

Intransigent: unwilling or refusing to change one's views or to agree about something, refusal to compromise or to abandon an often extreme position or attitude/uncompromising. (Miriam-Websters online dictionary)

Looking at these verses today in Jeremiah I believe it's clear to be on the right path on this side of heaven we must be "intransigent" about our faith. Uncompromising that there is Only True God, His Holy Word is the anchor and source of Truth and that the only path to God is through His Son Jesus Christ!

God states clearly here in Jeremiah that anyone who forsakes God will be ashamed! If not while alive they certainly will be upon their death and facing God without the blood of Christ covering them at judgement! Horrifying thought!

We must be bold in our faith. And I believe we can be while still being approachable, conversational, and joyful. That only can happen because of the hope and faith in Christ that we possess as believers.

We must be "intransigent" about our faith, not allowing the slow pervasive erosion of our fundamental beliefs to occur through compromise and "wanting to please, pacify and not offend anyone."

Moth's are attracted to light not darkness. Fisherman in the time of Christ and still today in third world countries, hang lanterns out over the water on a pole from the side of their boat to attract fish into there waiting nets below.

Mise is said to have lived by the following motto from the Roman philosopher Virgil: "Tu ne malis, sed contra audentior ito", "Do not give in to darkness(evil), but fight even bolder against it."

As born again Christians we must share the hope of Christ with all, we need to emanate the light of Jesus to this ever more dark world!

Intransigent about our faith in Christ! Are we?

———————————

Reflect on your own faith and convictions. Are you standing firm in your beliefs, or have you allowed compromise or societal pressures to erode your commitment to God's truth? Consider the importance of being "intransigent" in your faith—uncompromising and steadfast, even when faced with opposition.

SEEK THE LIGHT

"Heal me, O LORD, and I shall be healed; save me, and I shall be saved, for You are my praise. Indeed they say to me, 'Where is the word of the LORD? Let it come now!' As for me, I have not hurried away from being a Shepherd who follows You......."

Jeremiah 17:14-16

LET THY WORLD COME!

It has got to be "easy street" to be the prophet, the only prophet, the lone voice to your own countrymen and nation that have left God for false gods and lies, right? Your countrymen know (or should know) the history of how God has always been there for them to rescue their nation and take care of His people.

Obviously that is an immensely tough task, that has brought Jeremiah persecution, ridicule and loneliness (he is likely not a sought after dinner guest on the socialite circle).

So what does Jeremiah do when he faces this pressure and persecution? Goes to God in praise filled prayer of course! That would be our first response, right?

Hopefully, it will become our first response if it isn't already. As we mature and grow in our walk with the Lord and we experience more of life with Him our relationship deepens, our clarity as to what matters becomes more razor sharp and clear. It is really all about Him!

I confess in my marriage as Susan was growing and deepening her faith faster than I was, I often resented the "hot topic/disagreement" boiling down to Christ. I too often blurted out some variation of the following sentence, "everything doesn't have to be about God, or Jesus or His Word". News flash dude, it is all about Jesus!!!

Well this slow learner had not seen the full light as of yet and I was causing a lot of undue and unnecessary frustration to my bride! Or as one lady told me one day in practice as she had concluded that her husband was the major stress source leading to her neck tension and resulting headaches, "I think my husband proves evolution is fact, because he sure behaves like some knuckle dragging slow thinking subhuman creature often."

We are asking for teaching moments and training opportunities to learn it's all about Jesus when we are fighting His work in our lives, resisting the Holy Spirits' promptings and teachings in our life.

In my experience as we resist God we get short and irritable in our responses, flippant and cocky in our behavior and really down right ugly and prideful. Like Jeremiah's childish countrymen here in verse 15, "Where is the word of the LORD now Jeremiah? I am not seeing it, nothing happening yet?" (my paraphrase). I picture them saying this like a little child with their hand on their hip and sticking their tongue out when finished.

Jeremiah's calm, confident and mature response? "I have not left God or my tough calling to be your unappreciated shepherd you insolent bunch of immature, child like behaving 'adults.'"(again my paraphrase)

Let us always walk closely with God everyday, stay grounded in His Word, and never again put God in our back pocket!

It really is ALL about Him!

Identify a specific area in your life where you've been resisting God's work or struggling to see His hand at work. Write it down and pray over it daily, asking God to help you trust in His timing and plan, even when it's not immediately visible. Use this as an opportunity to deepen your faith and to remind yourself that, in every situation, it truly is all about Him.

LET THY WORD COME!

_____

_____

_____

_____

_____

_____

_____

_____

_____

_____

_____

_____

_____

_____

"As for me, I have not hurried away from being a shepherd who follows You, nor have I desired the woeful day; You know what I have what came out of my lips; Do not be a terror to me; you are my hope in the day of doom."

Jeremiah 17:16:17

Jeremiah 17:16:17

YOU ARE MY HOPE, OH GOD!

How quickly do we, or have we given up on God in our life? I know I could have done a better job throughout my life many times. I gave up praying for that lost person, quit sharing gospel/Christ nuggets with a lost friend or acquaintance. I know developing the pattern of going to God immediately for the tough things, and also going to Him in praise for all the good He has given is a "skill" that I need to hone and sharpen everyday for the rest of my life. To become a prayer warrior who never stops praying for the lost!

Going to prayer and seeking Him faithfully and diligently is not weakness, it is strength!

Opening the Bible much more often for His guidance, His purpose, His refreshment, His hope should be as habitual as breathing.

We should take no pleasure in seeing people who live a life of open rebellion against God who are headed to a godless eternity in Hell literally taunt God and sit back and say "well you asked for it person" and sit back and watch. These are the folks who literally taunt God in their rebellion, some actually saying, "so if your're really alive God and do exist, zap me, I dare you."

Jeremiah didn't take pleasure in their impending destruction, he was concerned for the souls and faithfully served God as bold witness!

Let us never hurry away from God! Stand firm!!!

———————————————

Reflect on your persistence in prayer and faithfulness to God. Have there been times when you've given up too soon on praying for someone or sharing your faith because the results weren't immediate? Consider how Jeremiah's commitment to his calling, even in the face of great opposition, can inspire you to remain steadfast.

As you stand firm in your faith and persevere in prayer, let your life reflect the unwavering hope and trust in God that Jeremiah exemplified, knowing that He is your strength and hope in all circumstances.

YOU ARE MY HOPE, OH GOD!

"Let them be ashamed who persecute me, but do not let me be put to shame; let them be dismayed, but do not let me be dismayed. Bring on them the day of doom, and destroy themwith double destruction."

Jeremiah 17:18

GOD IS OUR AVENGER!

Jeremiah reinforces that he doesn't need to bring about his revenge on all those who have attacked him and persecuted him, God will!

The King James Bible states: "Let them be confounded who persecute me…" this literally means to put to shame, be ashamed, be disconcerted, be disappointed. Jeremiah is asking God to turn the tables 180 degrees on those who are attacking him at every turn. Sounds like a reasonable request, doesn't it?

Have you ever witnessed, someone (maybe yourself) getting picked on, or harassed by the "bully" and then the tables get turned and the playing field leveled?

I confess I thoroughly enjoyed it when it happened to me! I was in third grade and went to sit down on one of those little metal legged plastic chairs at my desk. Just as I went to sit, Eric P. (class screw ball and rebel without a clue) pulled out my chair from under me and I went right down to the floor hard! It hurt and yes I cried, double humiliation.

Well guess who else saw it happen? My teacher, Mrs. Pfifer, that little lady was only about 4'10" tall but that day she was a giant!!

She marched back to Eric, levitated him out of his chair by his ear, marched him out into the hallway just outside the class door and proceeded to use her own "board/paddle" of education on his hind end. I am pretty sure his rear hurt more than mine.

But the best thing was that his wailing and crying in the hall was heard by my entire class and the entire second floor of Davenport Elementary!!!

Then to double emphasize her authority in that class room. She marched Eric back into the room (still firmly held by the ear) stood him in front of the entire class and told everyone that is what will happen to them if they ever pull a stunt like that. She then slow marched (via his ear still) Eric back to my desk to have him ask me directly if I was ok and made him apologize loud enough for the whole class to hear! Mrs Pfifer was my hero that day! She brought about double destruction on that goof ball. It was a beautiful thing!

DISMAYED, Disheartened; deprived of courage. (Websters 1828)

I could clearly understand how Jeremiah could become disheartened and totally zapped of his courage, couldn't you? Constantly being torn down, ran off, publicly ridiculed by the very people you are trying to wake up and bring to repentance before God hands out His wrath upon them!

Hang in their brothers and sisters in Christ, hold the line, don't back down, do not become dismayed, God is coming back and He will vindicate all injustices all inequities!

Mrs. Pfifer even decades later, earned my respect that day (she had already had it before the chair ordeal) and never lost it. It still amazes me to this day how tall she appeared to me.

God is coming to take care of business just as Mrs Pfifer did that day!

———————————

Reflect on your reactions when you face persecution or unfair treatment. Do you trust God to handle justice, or do you find yourself wanting to take matters into your own hands? Consider how Jeremiah's faith in God's justice can guide you to remain steadfast and avoid dismay in the face of adversity.

GOD IS OUR AVENGER!

_____

_____

_____

_____

_____

_____

_____

_____

_____

_____

_____

_____

_____

_____

_____

_____

RATIONAL RUMINATIONS

JEREMIAH | VOLUME I

Dr. Michael Detweiler

www.ingramcontent.com/pod-product-compliance
Lightning Source LLC
Chambersburg PA
CBHW060939120626
46557CB00003B/1058